I Thirst

Jacob Curran

Self-Published using Ingram Spark
December 2024

ISBN: 979-8-218-54325-9

Charcoal Drawings by Emma Engel

Index

Foreword

As I compile a collection of poetry called *I Thirst*, I can't help but feel a little vulnerable. In a way, this has been a long time in the making. The following poems are what I think to be the best of over 10 years of artistic endeavor. Throughout that time, I never knew I would keep at it though. There were many times where I was embarrassed of writing poetry, considering it effeminate in my adolescence and then counterproductive in my early twenties. It was hard to justify the usefulness of my poems to myself, let alone a meaning it might have to someone else.

Incidentally, it all feels a little obscene. *I Thirst* is expressive. Instead of aiming at a high, universal truth, it centers around some of the deepest longings of my heart and what it feels like to see those desires go unfulfilled. It reaches into my dark side and occasionally confesses aspects of myself that I take no pride in. Sometimes, I am unsure those things should be shared or publicly available. What have I to gain by tearing open my cloak and showing the world my naked chest? What have you to gain by looking at it?

In the spirit of apology, I will say that many of the darker, negative writing comes from periods of intense conversion and healing in my life. They put words to suffering, trying to make sense of the seeming void of meaning this world pretends to. A lot of these poems came more naturally to me than everyday speech, pouring out of me like water from a glass. They had to be expressed somehow and they found their form in the rhyming words collected here. They exist now as scars on these pages, remembrances of times when I was alone, when I didn't understand God, when I felt spurned or rejected.

I have intended in the movements of this collection to depict a fallenness, a death even, that is redeemed by a hope for resurrection. Thus, this collection is divided into four sections: an image of romance hoped for (I), a picture of the failure of that illusion (II), the reflection of that failure in other parts of the person, especially his spirit (III), and an exhortation in faith and hope to the providence of God, who is love (IV). There is a connection between these pieces, however tangential, that points from darkness to light. Do not interpret my sorrows as having any finality over me. My world does not consist of despair but hope for a new life, a perfect existence beyond this mortal plane.

In *I Thirst*, I speak the truth as I know it. I hold nothing back. I put myself on the page. I share in hopes that lovers, loners, people of conviction, guilt and freedom, doubt and faith can find themselves in these words, that they too can recognize their thirst for Charity and have hope in Love Penultimate to quench it. This world is dry and parched, thirsting for mercy. Let *I Thirst* be the finger's tip of water that ensures your perseverance toward the life to come, perfect, whole, just and true.

I

Good Side

I want to be on your good side so bad.

Lay down my life,

Let go of my desires if they lead me from you,

A lifelong fast, a repentance that never ends,

A fire that scorches me until you return

And restores what we had –

All of these I endure for your favor.

I would burn forever if the two of us could be.

Do you see what I endure? Hear me now?

For what seems like all my days

I have felt my lungs crying out to you

And somehow I hear nothing but silence.

You are svelte in that silence,

Coy because I've hurt you,

And Truth is not so easy to pursue.

The Watchman

Adoration after hours –
You feign asleep, your vigilance
Is expressed by crooked palms
Clutching at an empty bed.

Motionless I stand,
My hands cold as any dread,
As the terrors of the night,
That might kill your loneliness.

In the silence I can see,
You're yearning just to feel
The smooth of my skin sink in,
The touch of my hands on your hips.

I watch you twitch as if you heard
My long and solemn sigh.
You do adore me in the dark,
But will you love me in the light?

The Altar and the Offering

You strip me of my cleverness.
My tongue is tied in knots.
Every time I try to talk to you
I'm strange to my own thoughts.

There is a type of speechlessness,
A stillness you inspire,
Your society is sanctity
That sets my skin on fire.

We could pray together nightly.
We could dance in the flames.
We could marvel in the quiet
Or untie knots of shame.

You're a place of adoration,
An altar for the fire.
I am the gift, the offering
The holocaust[1] requires.

---

[1] *Ref. to an article called, "Holocaust in the Ancient World," describing the original meaning of the word, "holocaust"*

In my Mind

In my mind I'm in that airport
10,000 miles away,
Fighting to stay awake
Because you just said
What I always wanted to hear.

With my final breaths
I'll hold you to your words.
I'm laying on the floor.
Your hands twist the strands of my hair.
You promise you will write.

You think that I forgot.
I hold onto every word you said.
I let the letters live[2]
'til I can hear those words again.

---

[2] *Ref. Matthew 5:18*

All of Me

Every breath, every dream,
Every word written in ink,
Every whisper, every cry,
Every single solemn sigh,
Rich or poor, strong or weak,
Worn down by each aching need,
Lively like the first of spring,
Or feverish with body heat –
All of these I give to you,
All I am and all I do,
And if ever I fall short
Speak of what
You're yearning for.

Faith

I rely on her to love me
When the world grows cold.
She's a bet as safe as winter.
She is wealth as good as gold.

She lets my lungs breathe easy,
Because I know that she'll be there.
When my world falls all to pieces,
She buffers against despair.

Steadfast and faithful,
She wants to stand by me.
She's the woman that I love,
The one that gives me peace.

Fashion Show

Master of her mystery –
She contemplates the velvet dress,
Crosses the room to get to me,
She spins and I'm obsessed.
She sees the fruit of beauty,
She's pleased with her success:
A smile on my face
My hands upon my chest.

She turns from me, she walks.
Each step falls to the beat.
She returns to her closet.
She is going on retreat,
Meditating on the pieces
That conceal the world from me.
She's a master of the modest.
She maintains the mystery.

Far Side

My love lives on the far side of reason.
It is a fantasy, a dream
Way beyond good and evil.
In every season, every time
Other daydreams turn to dirt.
Tried and true, proven still
My love for you forever burns.

Instead of ash it is affection,
Never old and always new.
The glowing mantle is infectious.
The stony hearth resists the Earth–

Never dies, never dies,
It's always seeking its rebirth.
No sense disqualifies.
My love for you forever burns.

Trainwreck

A short dress, a tight skirt,
A V-Neck, a regret,
A jean jacket, high tops,
A wrist tat', some fishnets.

I love a good trainwreck
Leave it all a foul mess
Door unlocked, the lamp lit,
Shirt untucked, kitchen left
Disarrayed, your time spent
Telling me 'bout your ex –
Fifty shades of upset.

Spit it out, just confess
The late nights, the dm's,
A hot mess, a trainwreck.
Show me less than your best

Disarming

Dumb 'cuz I'm lovestruck
Love when you act tough
Dizzy in my head
When you catch me with that one look

I'm twigs and you're fire
Furnace of desire
Third degree burns
Let the flames fly higher

Your gaze is my weakness
Touch is my sweetness
I'd love to discuss
The things that you're thinking

Your beauty disarming
Affect is charming
You make me want
To give up what I'm guarding

Tear my defenses
Seek me relentless
And I will give breath
To these words of affection

Askew

When I look at you the world falls away.
It's fake or a farce or a waste of time
Designed to distract from the darling way
You crack a smile like a caution sign.
You look at me and it's sublime,
'Cuz I feel everything I ever knew
Denature and turn to dust in your eyes,
Two black holes take my life;
It's all askew,
'Cuz they're not black, they're brown
With gold flecks
Like stardust scattered across the sky
And I am a prospector.
These are pearls of price
Or crystal balls.
The future shown is mine.

Greed

He was born with a heart that nothing can please.
Choking on greed and gluttony,
It's more that he wants,
The beast that he feeds.

For grass that's green he sells meadows of gold,
His own soul.
His teeth rot and his skin bleeds.
He would give his life for a little more,

Another taste of excess,
Another seed of wealth sewn.
And what is more?
What is more?

More is the sunshine
And the breeze
And pause,
A moment to breathe,
A hand on his back.

His wife whispers, "Well done,"
And she stalls in the driveway.
Not a thing does she lack.

She checks her hair in the mirror and leaves.
She is beauty and she is all he needs.

Idol

To be so close to her
Constitutes a kind of blasphemy.
She knocks me to my knees,
But I can hardly pray
Because the words that I once used
To worship God I gave away
To another holy being
Whose name I'll never say.
I'm writhing in an agony that I cannot explain
'Cuz speaking more than small talk
Enslaves me to her name.
Her name, Lord, her name–
Speaking those sacred syllables
Would need to be in vain.
They'd weigh upon my conscience.
Lungs in my chest they'd strain.
The only word that can describe
The holiness of her acclaim
Is restricted from my speech.
If only I could say her name.

Hangover

Looking good but lights deceive me.
Brightest hues, reds and blues conceal
The beat, this song. The night is fleeting,
And she, the lie, the myth, stays with me.

Her make-up's streaking in morning light.
The colors bleed, the lines and hair dye
Are a live band's music out of time.
She's cacophony to sense of sight.

Pour cold and gray through window panes
And light the sheets where last night lays.

Surface Level Breach

Smoke rings and cyanide--
Who died tonight? I wonder.
What treasures are there left of you
That in the future I will plunder?
It's an old and worn out verse:
That everybody's awfully deep–
You're a trench of blood and pheromones
The depths of which I'll never reap–
But damn I feel good.
The water here is balm and bleach,
Warm enough for comfort,
But not too hot for me.
What'd be the point of sinking lower
Than this surface level breach,
And drowning in the chasms
Of confidential misery?
Please God, hide her secrets.
Let her remain a mystery.
Let her be known to you,
But never known to me.
I'm smoking to forget
All sensibility,
And dying to tread water,
Avoiding all familiarity.

Apology for not Texting Back
You are the kind of beautiful
That takes my words away.
I see you in my dreams at night,
No place I can escape.
You've got me deaf and dumb and blind–
I mean my mind is drawing blanks.
Every time I talk to you
I don't know what to say.

I am sorry I was late to text;
My fingers type too slow.
Got caught up in the strategy
Of conversation flow.
I wracked my brain for what comes next.
You thought that I left you on read.
I acted out but never meant
Apathy or ignorance.

Please don't try to read the silence
There's nothing there to see.
My love for you's like violence.
You mean the world to me.
If you said I had to claim it,
Speak to conquer and control,
I'm sure that I would find the words
And they would pour out of my soul.

Don't Forget

I can only hope you hate me,
That you clench your fists when you hear my name, its letters,
My face is scratched out of every postcard, every scrapbook,
Every Facebook status and photograph.

Show me that you cared
And torch it to the ground.
Let the flames rise,
The smoke climb to heaven as a holocaust,
An offering of what we could have had.
You poured your oil, your secrets, your hopes,
The best and worst of you into me,
And I deserted you.

Show me how it feels.
I want the tinder ashes,
The pile of rubble like the monument to charity.
Please, please hate me

Instead of playing you forgot,
Pretending you don't care,
Passing without so much as a nod,
Without eye contact.

I want the signature snarl,
The threat of your teeth
Digging into my vital arteries,
The stain of blood on the floor

Where I first said I love you.

Kill me –
Kerosene,
Blood and a pyre.

Melt the cold shoulder turned to you,
My frozen features,
With the fires of your wrath.
Burn away the frost with the rancor of love,
The inferno of passion,
But don't forget me.
God, please don't forget me.

Vanity Pangs

For my pridefulness to be the driving

Force behind my existence aggravates

My withered conscience, which shuns my striving,

My persistence down a path of ill fates

I am unprepared to stride alone or

With those who would sell me short of the ways

In which I am able to love,

And for that, Adriana, I should have kissed you

Years and years ago when I had the chance,

A decade now since my first love in those days

Failed to blossom into first romance.

What was born of that love or did it fade?

What comes now of my self preservation?

I am licking sores before they're open.

Cafeteria Cotillion & The Dark Night

I fear you like I fear the prom queen.
I'd never bother her;
Lunchroom Cotillion has her occupied.
I relish when she speaks to me–
Small talk, a smile in the hall–,

But never a long, cold night in two seats under the stars,
Speaking through each other,
A hundred miles down the lone, castoff streets
That no one ever cared enough to name.

I am setting up the gym for the dance,
Blowing up balloons and hanging streamers,
Never hoping for as much as romance,
Just that she will notice and that maybe

You will invite me to sit close to you,[3]
That for just one dark night,[4] I can have you.

---

[3] *Ref. Luke 14:10*
[4] *Ref. to wiki article on The Dark Night of the Soul*

Daughter of the Internet
She's a daughter of the Internet.
Formed by memes and chat-roulette.
Her mind lacks originality.
She conforms to unreality.
She's a daughter of the internet,
Goddess of her environment.

Sucker for a Savior

She's a sucker for a savior
Seeking silken linens,
Stained glass and sin
To make her bed with,

Sweet talk and cheap redemption,
Cause for her confession
To conference Catholic confidants;
Coffee hour is in session.

Holes in his hands: they're obsessed with,
Pouring over each wound of his–
All the words he speaks are blessing
To step further from the love of God
And into his possession,

But he's a devil not a saint,
He's a demon dressed in white.
Out of sight and out of mind,
He's out to take her life.

Sign the dotted line,
And melt into his hands.
Everything that made her shine
Dims like grains of sand,

Falling in the hourglass
Faster and faster,
Til the glass is overturned
And the blood's on both their hands.

Samson and the Paramour

I am Delilah,

Continents away from you,

My beloved Nazirite.

With the scattered beats of the city behind,[5]

Amidst the roar of urban chaos

I forget my God for my love of wealth.

I am hidden from my own affections.

Come.

Find me in the tallest tower

Pouring over spreadsheets to feed my family.

Concrete pillars of a temple, they are

Built for the worship of some unholy god–

Paramour that I pay homage to,

Who feeds me when I plow his field,

Who nurtures seeds of my resentment

And loves my distraction,

My blindness at work,

Who loves when my ears are stone deaf and cold,

When my vocal cords do not ring out.

---

[5] *Ref. to "Hey there Delilah" by The Plain White T's*

Sing to me Samson.
Do not relent until I turn to you,
Faithful and free.
Leave no stone unturned, no idol unbroken.
Never again let your melodies cease
Until every bone of mine is covered
In sinew and flesh,
The means of movement,
Until pulse of life is rediscovered.
Let the thrum of your voice, and beat of the drum
Rattle the base of this sanctuary,[6]
And should I die as it crumbles to dust
Should I be extinguished with all that I know,
With the destruction of greed and false prosperity,
Hold me close to you, my love.
Let me feel heat of your breath on my skin
And your arms around me one last time.

---

[6] *Ref. to Samson of Judges 13-16*

Static

There's a barrier between you and me,

A gray mass in my mind to keep me blind

From light of the sun that might shine between

The branches of the trees that died when light left the world,

When the winter storm began,

And it seemed as if it would never cease.

Freezing rain poured through the sky above

And the heavens were masked with seeming ease

By the sound of static and sight of gloom.

Everything you've said or done is obscured from me.

Instead of your words I hear doom resounding.

I can't see you and I'm scared

That I might never feel your touch again,

That you might never speak to me again.

Lost

Take back your memories – let me lose myself.
Let me forget my fear.

I'm fading fast, like the photographs on your shelf.
The poses staged fade now into the past,
Like me, a flask of wax,
Melting with each moment,
Dripping from the candlestick
Without precision,
Without urge to reach out to you
To cleanse me of the filth
That separates my heart from yours.
No want wells within me.
So what am I to do?

Ask for the wax to never melt
Or haunt myself with pictures of the past,
Me with you standing over my shoulder,
Telling me who I am,
Soothing me with your charity?

III

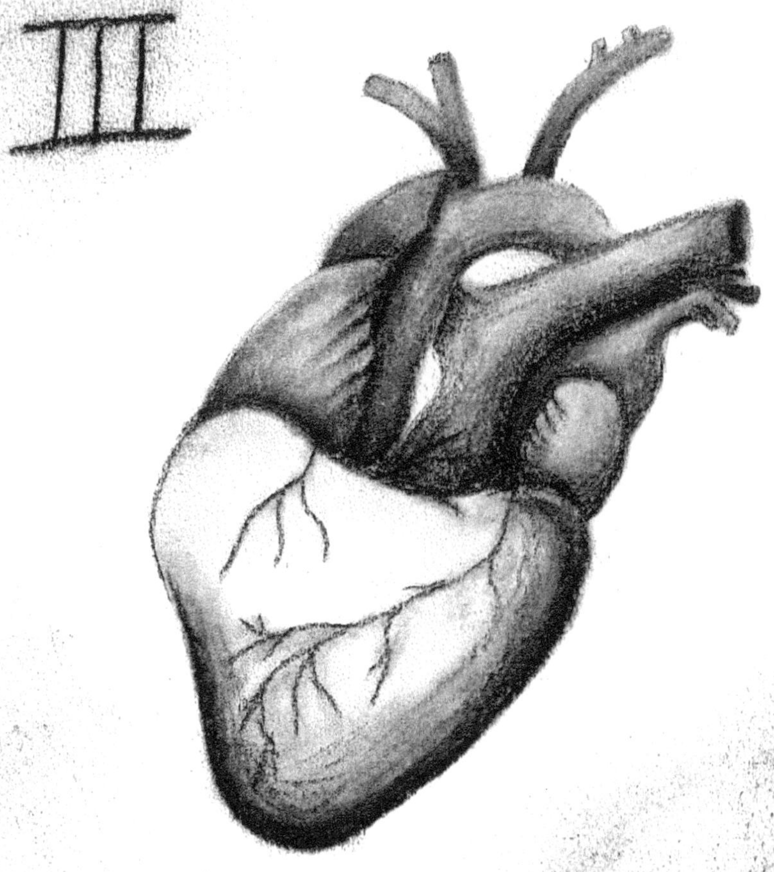

blasé

There's nothing to say on days like these.

The sun may find its sleep in the west, blazing each day from the

east.

It may have rained today but no sense of change or water falling

struck me with feelings distinct.

Neither conflict nor sensation gave me lasting peace.

All I want is to see the difference between now and then,

To discern the passing seasons, to feel breeze

In my hair or to fall asleep

Near someone who makes me feel something,

Whose weathered face I can count the age lines on.

Instead my bed is empty,

And I am incomplete.

Empty

Empty

Nothing gnawing

Grasping in men

Who chase after things that murder

Lonely

Rent's Rising

Iron door slams shut.
Mother flees from her nest in fear.
Her child roots for warmth,

A ring of flowers.
Chicks shiver between the twigs.
Flesh roots for its source.

Out of sight for days
I shudder to think she left
And for good this time.

Why build home so close
To the evil ones; risk it
For floral baskets?

Death anxiety –
The cost of prime real estate.
The chicks must be cold.

Indecision

Days may disappear and the weeks roll by.
In the blink of an eye passing before you
Is the hand of time without care for right or wrong you've done,

And you feel a fool
For thinking you could cheat it,
Beat the night at its own game.

Its claws tear into you and your skin falls from your face in rolls
Like saddlebags that hit the floor,
Like a soup of sins you could not help but to taste,
Like death at your door, knocking, patiently waiting
Because it hears in your breath haste for your final moments.

Away wasting you lay on your bedside and count the minutes in
a dark room.
What on Earth will you do?

Fritter Away

Fritter away at the edge of oblivion
The days pass like wind and you are oblivious
Your god counts the seconds until years pass you by
And at the end of it all your time will have come
Now it all comes crashing down around you
And the skies lay limply at your ankles

Look back at the months meshed together in one gray mass
Every word of his spent trying to make ends meet
Each day, hour, minute grinding you down to a pulp
His temple remains four white walls and a pile of rugs
There is a clock on the wall sounding out time stamps
Without fail, without wavering, without ceasing,
Without putting aside time to awaken his child
Who waits patiently for the breath of new life

Shadow

Evil on evil, throw stone upon stone.
Take measure for measure my flesh and blood.
Place on my shoulders the weight of the world.
Task me with completing impossible work.

Find me in the shadows, waiting for light,
Wailing like I won't be brought to new life.
Sorrow, it stirs you, at last you see
Bodiless image of glory to be.[7]

Please call on my name; commend me to peace,
Or else I'm condemned forever to be
A spirit perturbed, a specter of night,
Never allowed to pass from this life.

---

[7] *This is a poem from the POV of a ghost. Church Tradition teaches that if ghosts exist they are souls of the dead, stuck in purgatory, waiting on the prayers of the faithful to purify them so they can be released into heaven.*

Cryogenic-Gothic[8]

I'm dead to you I guess
It's obvious to see
The light has left my eyes
You point to graying in my teeth
The cheeks have lost their pout
You say the lungs have breathed their last
By your word my heart has stopped
And my flesh is dying fast
But dig a little deeper
Find that I'm still alive
The cold that I've embraced
Has protected my insides
And as soon as winter ends
I'm sure that you will see
The necessity of death
To live eternally

____

[8] *Ref. "Cryogenic Gothic" on the link tree for a Facebook post which contains the idea that inspired this poem*

I Thirst[9]

Kneeling over the body,

Scooping fistfuls of flesh in my mouth,

Is it my fault I'm constantly in need?

What good is perpetual thirst?

Is it me or God who's unsatisfied?

Can hunger be said to err?

Ripping a hole through my insides

Only the vacuum is clear,

Wishing only to edify,

To make it known there is life,

Organic matter I can imbibe.

Cups of cannibals[10] never run dry.

Though we engorge on the holy one's body,

Though the yoke of our love is a curse,

Though our Lord is in love with his righteousness,

Such that our bodies belong in the dirt,

So that the stench may never reach heaven

Of perfection run its course

Purify me,

Sanctify me,

Glorify me, Lord.

---

9 *Ref. Psalm 63*
10 *Ref. Defending the Cannibals - Early Christians were thought to be cannibals for claiming to eat the body and blood of Christ.*

You thirst for the blood that you gave me,[11]
And someday soon I will give it,
But I have to know you will save me
From the depths of a love that starves Christians.[12]

---

[11] *Ref. John 19:28*
[12] *Ref. Romans 8:22*

Will Wait

I will wait.

I will starve to death in this palace of stone,

This fortress of solitude,

This cemetery graveyard,

This mountaintop,

This highrise, my coffin,

This fast food drive through, my final stand.

I will thirst and thirst,

Persist in desire in alleyways and deserts

And strip malls and meadows.

In the airport I am lost.

I speak my last words and expire.

In the Vatican I am on the verge of death

Yearning desperately to separate from my skin

And join in the Holy Communion.

It is silent in this sanctum.

My mind is a steady din.

My heart beats as the seconds pass

And my flesh burns with desire.

I am who I am

And I will keep wanting.

St. Dismas

Bleed with me, babe.
Taste my lips turn sour.
A reed will reclaim
Sickness I've devoured.

Sucking the wine
Out of sponge on a reed,[13]
Succumb have I
To God's grace. I'm replete

With gifts that he's given
To my sorry face
At the expense
Of an unfavoured race.

You have been asked
To bear the weight of my grief,
To untie the knots
Of Adam and Eve,

Forgiving my sins
And wiping my cheeks
Of the tears I have wept
In hopes that I'd seize

---

[13] *Ref. John 19:29*

A piece of the heavens,
Light gone unseen,
Since bound in the dark,
Held in captivity.

One thing I've learned,
Through toil and strife,
Is for one to live
Another must die.

Your wounds leak now,
While my blood has dried,
And as you send up your sighs,
Mourning and weeping,

I've paid heed to my weakness.
It's wine I've been drinking.

Workshopping "Song of Myself" with Walt Whitman[14]

Holy shit...

That's cool.

Sorry, I just felt like I had to say that before we move on,

The image of a hunter falling asleep next to his dog and gun after

a successful day.

It just hits right, y'know?

The way poetry should hit a reader.

Okay...

So there's a ship...?

You're settling new land...?

No, you're watching a wedding?

How can you be a hunter, a sailor, and have time to entertain slaves?

Who are you trying to be Walt?

What exactly are you saying you are?

Here you claim the Earth to yourself, but what does that even mean?

Does the dirt respond to your action potential? Does the grass

twitch at your fingers' touch?

Who of us can claim the cry of fire is who he is?

Go back with me, Walt.

Arouse that sleeping hunter.

Tell me what stories the twilight speaks to him.

Tell me the way he,

-The way you-, feel safe in the company of your canine.

---

[14] *Ref. "Song of Myself" by Walt Whitman*

Maybe something like,
"Without that dog, without my rifle I am nothing,
The woods eat, sweat and breathe without me,
Enveloping any man who signs its contract,
Entering into contention with oblivion."
I don't know, something along those lines.

You've got a lot to say.
You're one of those writers who can capture everything under
the sun
In a single inkblot.
So speak to me, Walt.
Tell me who you left behind to conquer the wilderness
To feel the grease of a feral beast drip from your lips
Onto your scraggly beard.

And for your readers' sake, stay still
Self-obsessed glutton
Even if that means you must sleep.
Don't abandon me to distal shores
Allow me to feel the heat of the fire,
To harmonize with the crickets' chirping,
And to feel the weight of the rabbit meat
As it falls through my esophagus into my intestine-
Before you steal away,
Before your restlessness would leave me so dissatisfied.

A god is holy when it takes its time
To sit and explain to its subjects the stars one by one,
When the fruit of its vine is elevated to the
experience of all its flavors,
All its dastardly worries and wants,
All its victories and vicissitudes
And especially all the tiny moments in between
Those disaffected instances of contemplation
That lead a person back to the ground
On which he was standing all along.

In this piece, you call your Self The God,
But the whole time I'm listening to you, I'm spinning.
My appetite waxes when you mention a lover's arms,
A warm meal, the multitudes you contain,
And wanes when you leave me pining in the grass
Where there are contradictions
Where there is wailing and gnashing of teeth.
If you will be my God, Walt,
Wait with me.
Talk with me.
Dine with me.
Because I'm the one who has to read this shit.

Insomnia

It's the love of God

That keeps me up at night

To remind me that I lose my life

Every time I compromise

On the dream of paradise.

Depictions of the devil wake

Me from the rest that might erase

Sins I committed yesterday

When yesterday was only yesterday.

It's God that pulls me from my sleep,

Shows me the nightmare in the dream.

Bathed in sweat, between the sheets,

The Ghost turns slumber into screams.

A chainsaw in a concrete cell,

The acid vats, they sear and swell,

Eroding all my hope to dwell,

To languish in the depths of Hell.

Attacked by men I gave my trust,

Seen those I love reduced to dust,

These dreams designed by wrath and lust

Keep me awake.

Keep me awake.

Wash me clean and keep me dry

Lord who says that sleepers lie[15]

To themselves and those they love.

---

[15] *Ref. Romans 13:11-12*

It's said at night[16]
The thief
He comes.

---

[16] *Ref. Matthew 24:43, John 10:10*

Anesthesia

I see it sometimes in dreams,
In bits and pieces on TV screens,
In scenes of my life I would skip.

It shows me glimpses for pain.
For the price of my life,
Every dollar and dime will pay
For a sneak peek, a respite
From what's real that's too hard to face.

That paradise takes sacrifice.
So hush now; take a deep breath.
Relax your whimpering form,
And let the sweetness of dreams pour

Like anesthesia into your skull.

oasis

today

I am faced with the curse of my filth

I am confronted with the image

of a pool

centered in a clearing

in a forest

the forest is

dark, overgrown

the roots of the trees overwhelm one another

and the moss leeches the life they would otherwise have

people gather at the pool

crawling

their legs paralyzed with fear

or some other disease,[17]

made to crawl on their bellies

to the oasis

the water is clear

there is a fountain at the center

people have been gathering at the pool for as long as anyone can

remember

and most of those who show up repeatedly

have been hooked since the first time they used it to bathe

they come filthy

and walk away clean,

---

[17] *Ref. John 5:5, John 5:1-9*

the pool no dirtier than it was
before they washed
the filth they accumulate simply
returns to the earth,
floats gently to the bottom of the pool

I wish I could find this pool
but I am without guidance
I wish I could wash myself
but my flesh is stubborn
I wish for counsel from one who is washed
but how can I tell who is worthy
the dirt accumulates so quickly
underneath their fingernails

Stuck

you contain me in my home,
alone, away from distractions
that might dismiss the fog, might show
a way back to you, direction
I might take, a path, the beaten
road that will take me from the dark
into the light, from confusion,
from meandering phrase to stark
depiction of truth, from mundane
to meaning, from thick fog to rain

the water of new life

The Fourth Cup

Allow me to drink from the cup I'm given,[18]

Especially if it's sour,

So that I may enjoy that which is sweet

In the breaths of my final hour.

---

[18] *Ref. Matthew 20:20-23, Matthew 26:39*

Reconciliation

Until you show your face
I'll pretend I know what's love,
Make believe the curses that are spit
Remove from my eyes dust and mud.
The distance from you that I feel
I'll believe that I deserve,
And despite my earthly sorrows
I'll have faith in every word
In enumerations of the shame
With which I am neatly dressed.
I'll count you blameless for the times
I was conquered with unrest.
Reconcile me to your care
And let me beg for love.
Let me cry for visit from
You who I've been calling on.

Pharisee

I feel like a hypocrite,[19]
So far beneath my own critiques,
Entombed I am in secrecy,
Such that I can barely breathe.

I've made my home among the righteous.
My heart of stone has found a seat
In sepulchers[20] of the highest,
The holiest society–

---

[19] *Ref. Matthew 23:13*
[20] *Ref. Matthew 23:27-28*

Valley of Bones– it hears no thunder.[21]
The hills of corpses turn their cheeks.
The voice of God resounds in longing;
He lost us to the law he keeps.

Breathe away the bitterness.
Let the wind increase in speed.
Let my bones and ligaments
Find a heart that beats.

And while the earth in frenzy spins
In a storm of flesh and bone,
Assure each muscle finds its place
And each organ finds its home.

IV

The Hole in the Stone and the Marital Debt[22]

Have mercy on these old walls,
A hole in the stone I am,
A cave in the Holy City.
Wipe away the gossamer
And take your rest here.
I yearn for the body.

I am frozen with the years,
Rigid as the bones of Cain,
Inert since the death of this world.
The best of me is carved away
To make room for the body.

I am dark and damp and full of filth,
But for these three days I am yours.
Not a palace but a portal,
Not a temple but a tomb,
I am the final courtesy of the living,
The hole in the Earth that needs sealing.

---

[22] *Ref. to The Temple of the Holy Sepulchre's wikipedia page*

Do not fear the scent of herbs, of myrrh,
The stone that plugs my mouth.
Your destiny is beyond these walls,
But to hold you is my birthright,
My one hope, my salvation.

So lay here.

Give me the body
Until every stone sings,
Until the lips move,
And the rock walls cry out,[23]
"Hosana! Hosana! Hosana in the highest!"

A thousand years like three days—[24]
I'm sure you won't be long.

---

23 *Ref. Luke 19:40*
24 *Ref. 2 Peter 3:8 and Psalm 90:4*

Rage

Your rage
At the setting of the sun
Will be undone,
Will be undone.
All will be new.
All will refresh,
Like morning dew,
An ice cold rush,
Of water running
Down your back,
Soothing soreness,
Silver sickness,
The lack of just
One holy witness.
Your rock, your refuge,
Holy water–
He will return
Healing all,
And you will wipe your eyes[25]
One last time.

---

[25] *Ref. Revelation 21:4*

Imitating Kenosis[26]

Sprawled on the floor - I will eat dirt for you.

The earthworm and rat are my companion.

I am a speck of dust paying it's due.

My pride, my ego - let me abandon,

Because you are gold and I am silver.

You are the master and I am the slave.

You are an oak and I am a sliver.

I am a woman,

A lover who *craves* –

A perfect union of my heart with yours.

Banish separation between us.

I lay down in the muck and the mud

For hours, days, years,

As long as it takes the dust to know its place,

To know humility,

To know an ounce of love you have for me.

---

[26] *Ref. Philippians 2:1-11*

Adoration

The scent of incense in this room,[27]
A multitude of sparks of fire,
The candlesticks and gold illume
My love, the root of my desire.

My heart is burning at the sight.
My mind's aglow with flame from wick
Which melts away the dark of night;
It passes as the seconds the tick.

I lay face down on tiles of stone.
The walls resound with silence still.
I'm prostrate in this catacomb.
With adoration I am filled.

Despite accouterments of death,
The sacrificial victim's corpse,
The monstrance pulses with his breath.
His slow and labored love outpours.

---

[27] *Ref. the Linktree button titled, "Adoration" is a video of the chapel this was written in*

Rainier

I can see glimpses of the otherworld:
Every dozen miles the vista opens wide,
The bridal veil's torn,
Gift of God unfurled.

Like dancers,
Douglas Firs peel to the side,
Revealing the piles of stone, dirt and frost,
Reaching to the sky
Unlike anything made by the hands of men that is lost to time;
It all dies.

Now I feel the sting of my existence,
An ounce of dirt,
I'm no lover like the God who makes mountains.
I am a mere stone in this canyon,
I'm without words.
My little heart is pounding

At the signs and symbols of Neverland
This place made for me,
Crafted by his hand.

Thorn Bushes

FLIRT WITH IT
DISTURB THE EARTH – PROBE THE ROOTS – OF
THE PERVERSE – REVERSE IT – BREAK THE DIRT –
ENSURE THAT LIFE – DOES NOT RETURN

Garden bed in my chest
Festering with leafy pests
The weeds upturned and now undead
Threaten my concupiscence[28]

LIVE WITH IT – SPURN THE CURSE – THE HEART
LAID BARE – BY THE IMPURE – MUTATED –
IMMATURE – THE FRUIT OF GOD –
CHOKES THE HERB

---

[28] *Ref. CCC 2515*

Zacchaeus' Trunk

Everything I touch turns to dust
And withers away in the wind,
But one day above the rust
I will rise from the mud without sin
And freed from the chains of death
That laid me down to begin with,
Renewed by the holiest breath,
My flesh will renew and thicken
In the trunk of the sycamore.
My roots will take hold in the Earth,
And I will bend and break no more.
I will offer shelter and mirth
To he who climbs my body.
What he is seeking he will see.[29]

---

[29] *Ref. Luke 19:4, Matthew 7:7-8*

Roses' Red

Filter of the earth
Grey sheet slides across the sky
The greens are pulsing

Sheen of foliage
Roses' red defies the gloom
Not so blind as night

Breathe

Breathe new life and from the ashes raise me,

Bodily Sacrament primordial.[30]

Eons before humankind came to be

Spirit of love sought the corporeal.

It was the person of unity

That overcame the spirit of strife,

Worlds of disorder[31] brought to their knees

While the primeval was brought to new life.

It is the person of unity,

Holy Communion,

One flesh made by God,

-Marriage-

That brought all earthly things to be,[32]

Spirit and truth sent to reclaim the void.

In that formless void I wait.

For you, I do abide.

All that I am renew.

---

[30] *Ref. to Pope John Paul II's General Audience of 10/6/1982 on EWTN's website*

[31] *Ref. Genesis 1:2*

[32] *Ref. to NCR article about Theology of the Body*

The Waiting

Minutes before dawn when the wonderful night
Will come crashing down in scatters of light
Each brilliant hue of orange and red–
And what do we do just minutes before?

The miles we've traveled, the blood that we bled,
Each step that we took, while yearning for rest
Now one day away from our journey's end
What progress was there? What strain is there left?

With wasteland behind, the desolate night,
In these final moments of longing for light
We strive to remember the things that were said
How do we find ourselves at the world's edge?

Now the sun crests over the horizon
And we see what it is we hoped for

Mass

What kind of feast do we approach?

It's step by step and row by row.

The saints process all in a line,

Mouthful of blood, taste of the Light.

The wedding vows, blood sacrifice,

The bridegroom gives away his life.

Banquet begins, never to cease.

The dining hall shakes at the knees.

The blast of horns makes the walls quake.

The tongues of fire engulf in flames

A people offered up in praise.

A holocaust commemorates

The battle o'er, the victory won,

The death of God, his only son,

Thanksgiving now for all he gave.

From Satan's maw, mankind is saved.

Psalm 63[33]

O God, thou art my God;

early will I seek thee:

my soul thirsteth for thee,

my flesh longeth for thee

in a dry and thirsty land,

where no water is;

to see thy power and thy glory,

so as I have seen thee in the sanctuary.

Because thy lovingkindness is better than life,

my lips shall praise thee.

Thus will I bless thee while I live:

I will lift up my hands in thy name.

My soul shall be satisfied as with marrow and fatness;

and my mouth shall praise thee with joyful lips:

when I remember thee upon my bed,

and meditate on thee in the night watches.

---

[33] *This is not an original but it is referred to throughout this collection and it encapsulates the heart of what a lot of what this selection of poems is about.*

Because thou hast been my help,
therefore in the shadow of thy wings will I rejoice.
My soul followeth hard after thee:
thy right hand upholdeth me.

But those that seek my soul,
to destroy it, shall go into the lower parts of the earth.
They shall fall by the sword:
they shall be a portion for foxes.

But the king shall rejoice in God;
every one that sweareth by him shall glory:
but the mouth of them that speak lies shall be stopped.

Afterlife

At the dying of the light,
I will call upon thy name;
I will put thy soul to rest;
I'll exhume from thy remains

That initial spark in you,
Bulb of light that I did place,
In the caverns of thy heart,
In the joy upon thy face,

'Cuz although it waxed and waned
In the years you were alive,
It's purpose it has served.
You've come home, and so must I

Collect upon arrival
Sum total of thy feats.
My love is your revival.
Uncontrived love is my peace.

And at the dying of the light
When all is said and done,
When the book of life is closed,
I'll preserve what I have loved.

Support the Artist

There are many ways to love. For most seasons, one should hide himself, wait patiently for the moment he knows he is among friends and can open his cloak, can loosen the grip of his clutching hand on his pearls. There is a coldness and a certain professionalism in that demeanor but it must be. Wickedness can tell the signs and symbols of vulnerability from far off and a man's humanity is too precious for some other frivolousness or passionate naivety to rule his relationship toward it.

"I Thirst" does not follow this impulse. It follows another calling, the compulsions of another season.

In anticipation of the upcoming Jubilee Year of our Lord, I call upon hopes and disappointments, triumphs and failures toward the end of union with our God. *"I Thirst"* shares with a person the worlds of flesh I yearn for but cannot touch and the world of spirit that I cannot yet know. It is an offering, a private revelation shared which ideally prepares a person for the upcoming year. I hope for it to disrupt the cold, soften the stone, give attention to the breath of new life offered to him. Stiff and unmoving are we at best; dead to love at worst. We all need the heat.

If my words moved you in this way, please do as I have done and share them: email them to a friend, speak them privately to your God, carve them into a tree at the park, or share yourself: tell your lover a secret, dance, call a friend.

The artist looks for inspiration, goes to work and shares it, hoping its flame is kept in that transference well enough to light someone else's torch, to nudge the first spark, the flickering desire in their heart for something more, to a scorching inferno of passion. If *"I Thirst"* does not effect you to even the slightest generosity, does not push you to let go of yourself as I have here, then my nakedness in these pages is indecency, my efforts an echoing narcissism, a gray and lifeless vanity that I am tempted to regret.

Bio

Jacob Curran is a Catholic musician, poet, and father who has dedicated himself to exploring the depths of faith and human experience. Having moved around the U.S. as a military child, he has developed a unique perspective on life and spirituality. With a BA in English from the University of Washington, Seattle, he brings a literary sensibility to his poetry. His work often delves into themes of love, loss, and the search for meaning. Through his heartfelt and honest verse, Jacob invites readers to connect with their own spiritual journeys and find solace in the divine.

References

All sources of inspiration for my work cited in the text can be found here– (https://linktr.ee/3TEntertainment).